My Sight Word List

a	in	said
and	is	see
away	it	the
big	jump	three
blue	little	to
can	look	two
come	make	up
down	me	we
find	my	where
for	not	yellow
funny	one	you
go	day	
help	play	
here	red	
I	run	

Name: _____________ Date: _____________

Today is: | Monday | Tuesday | Wednesday |
| Thursday | Friday |

Direction: Trace and read the sentences.

| fun | gun | run | sun |

They are having fun.

He has a gun.

The bear is running.

The sun is smiling.

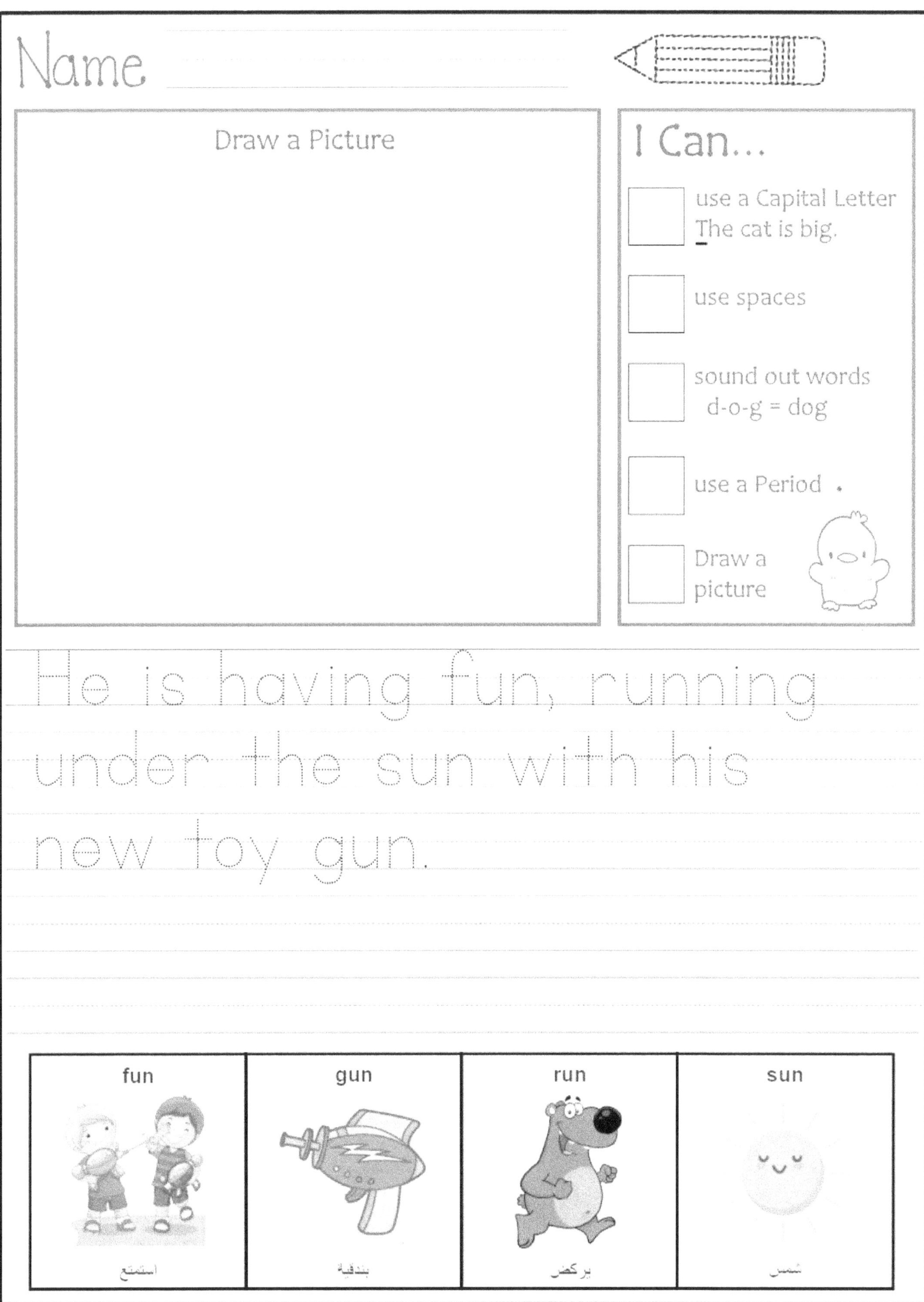
Name

Draw a Picture

I Can...

use a Capital Letter
The cat is big.

use spaces

sound out words
d-o-g = dog

use a Period .

Draw a
picture

He is having fun, running
under the sun with his
new toy gun.

fun

gun

run

sun

استمتع

بندقية

يركض

شمس

Name: ____________________ Date: ____________________

Today is: Monday Tuesday Wednesday Thursday Friday

Direction: Trace and read the sentences.

bag	rag	tag	wag

كيس	خرقة	بطاقة شعار	يهز

He has many bags.

I see a rag.

I see a tag.

Its tail is wagging.

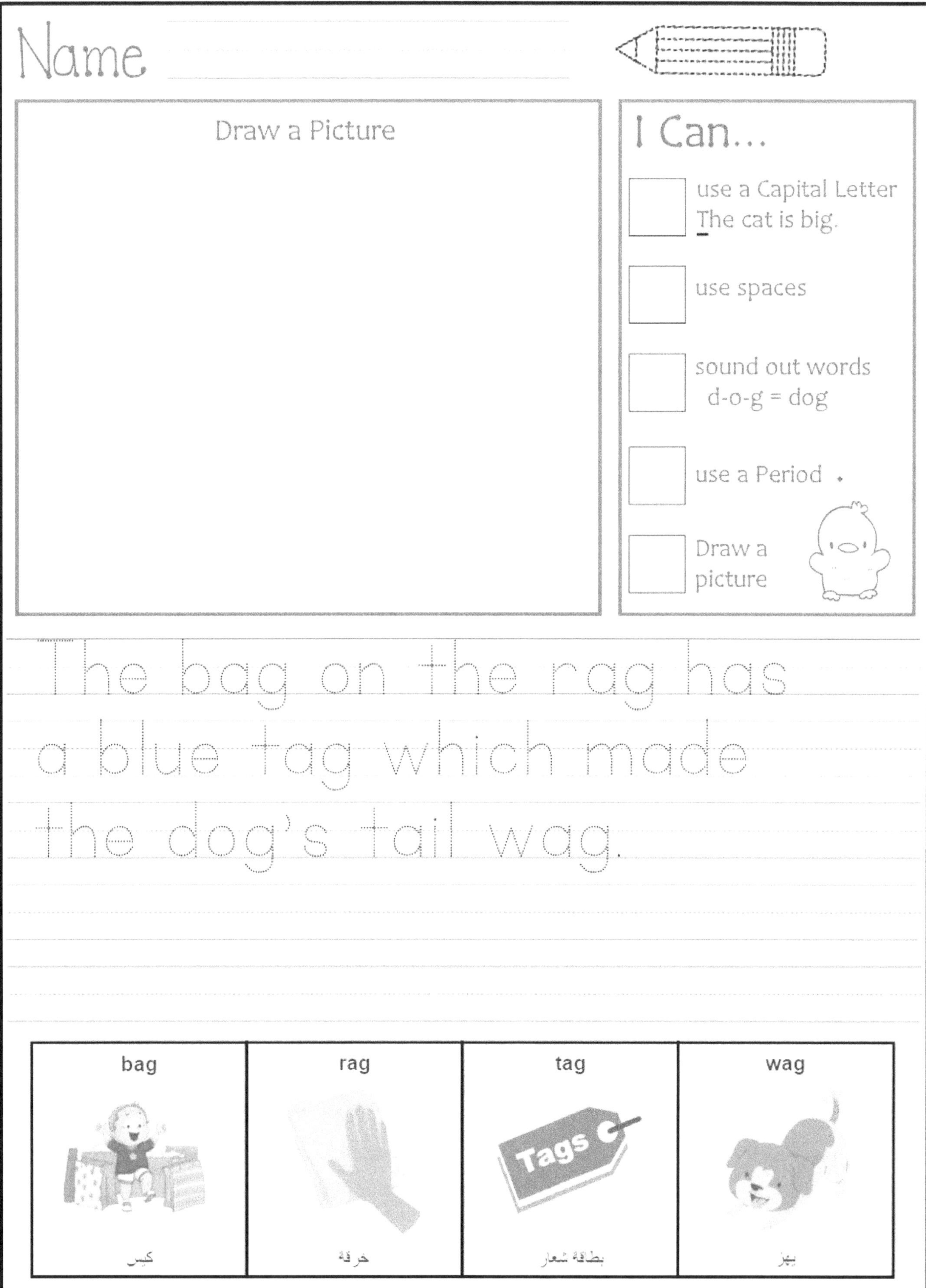

Name
Draw a Picture
I Can...
use a Capital Letter
The cat is big.
use spaces
sound out words
d-o-g = dog
use a Period .
Draw a picture
The bag on the rag has a blue tag which made the dog's tail wag.
bag
rag
tag
wag
كيس
قطعة قماش
بطاقة شعار
يهز

Name: _______________ Date: _______

Today is: [Monday] [Tuesday] [Wednesday]
[Thursday] [Friday]

Direction: Trace and read the sentences.

can	man	pan	van
علب	رجل	مقلاة	سيارة نقل

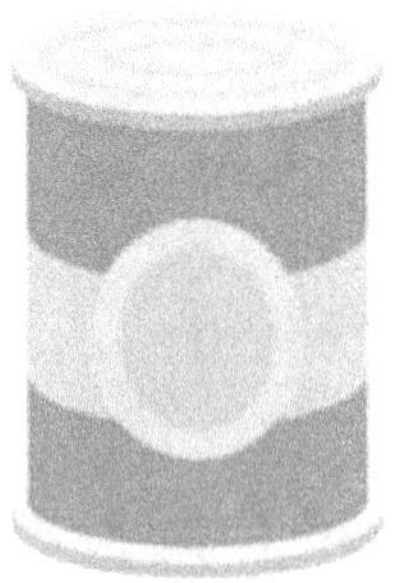

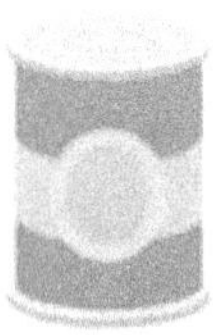

I see a can of soda.

The man is happy.

The pan is dirty.

I see a big van.

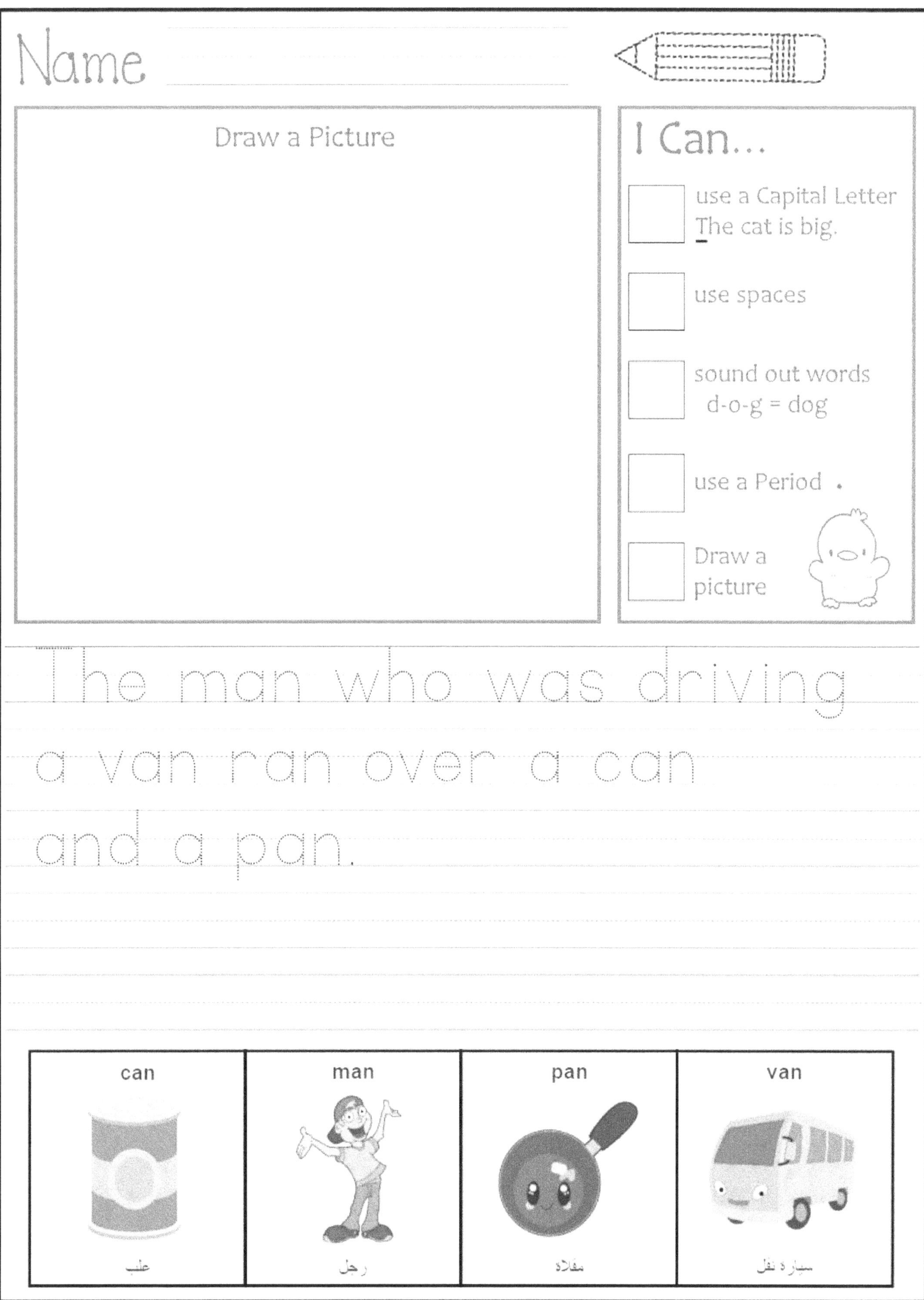

Name

Draw a Picture

I Can...

use a Capital Letter
The cat is big.

use spaces

sound out words
d-o-g = dog

use a Period .

Draw a
picture

The man who was driving
a van ran over a can
and a pan.

can
علبة

man
رجل

pan
مقلاة

van
سيارة نقل

Name: ______________________ Date: ______________________

Today is: Monday | Tuesday | Wednesday | Thursday | Friday

Direction: Trace and read the sentences.

cut	gut	hut	nut

يقطع	أمعاء	كوخ	البندق

He cut his nails.

He has a gut.

This is a small hut.

It is holding a nut.

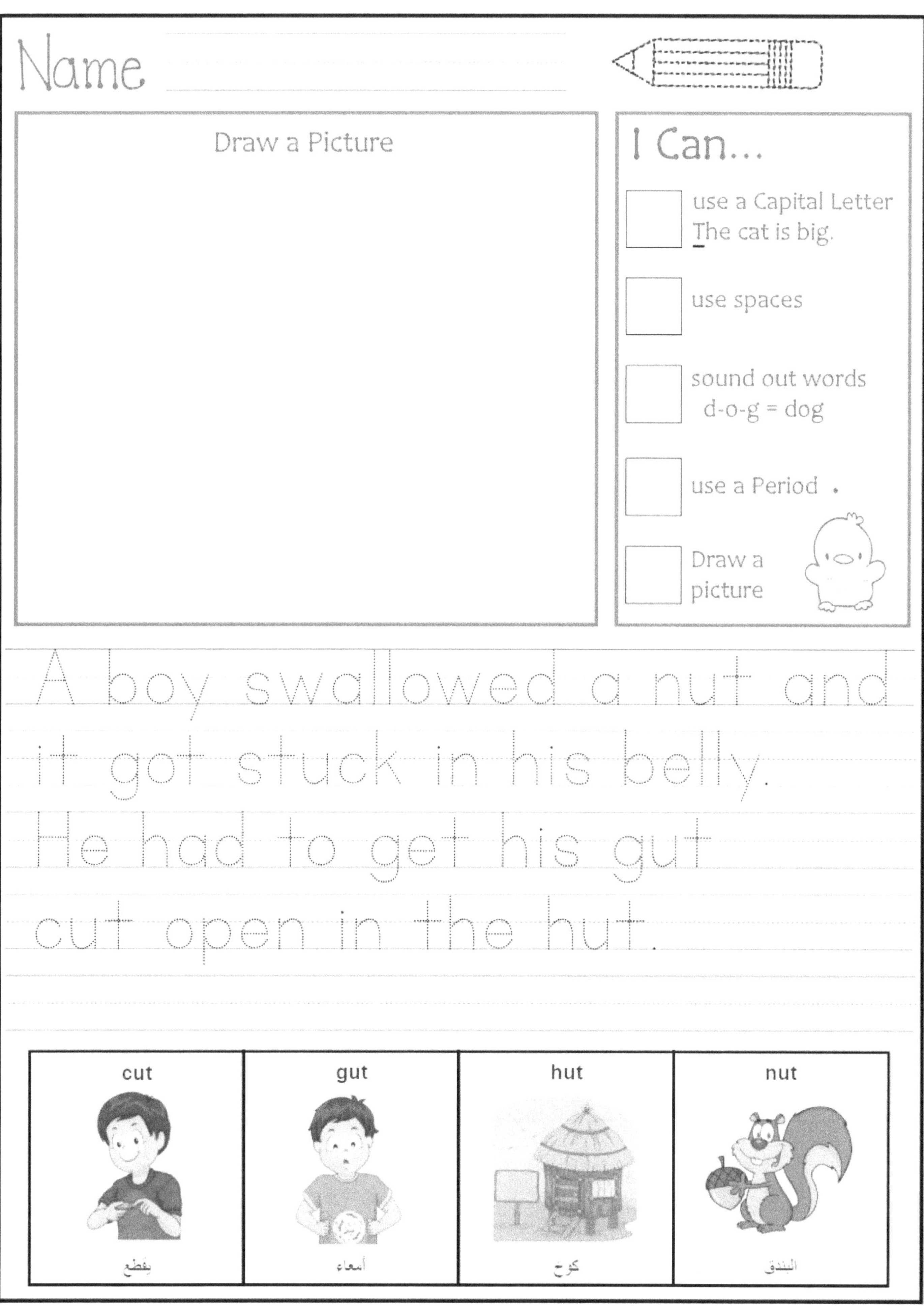

Name

Draw a Picture

I Can...

use a Capital Letter
The cat is big.

use spaces

sound out words
d-o-g = dog

use a Period .

Draw a
picture

A boy swallowed a nut and
it got stuck in his belly.
He had to get his gut
cut open in the hut.

cut
يقطع

gut
أمعاء

hut
كوخ

nut
البندق

Name: _________________ Date: _______________

Today is: | Monday | Tuesday | Wednesday |
| Thursday | Friday |

Direction: Trace and read the sentences.

| fat | cat | hat | mat |

I see a fat dog.

This is my little cat.

I like this hat.

I see a big mat.

Name _______________________

Draw a Picture

I Can...

- [ ] use a Capital Letter
  <u>T</u>he cat is big.
- [ ] use spaces
- [ ] sound out words
  d-o-g = dog
- [ ] use a Period .
- [ ] Draw a picture

The fat cat laid on the mat that was a hat pattern.

fat	cat	hat	mat
سمين	قط	قبعة	حصيرة

Name: ____________________ Date: ____________________

Today is: Monday Tuesday Wednesday Thursday Friday

Direction: Trace and read the sentences.

cab	lab	tab	crab
		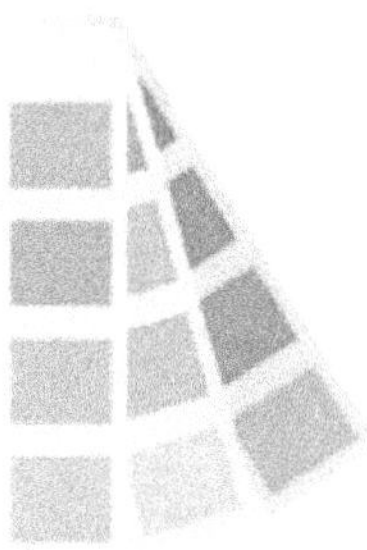	
سيارة أجرة	مختبر	التبويب	سلطعون

The cab is fast.

The lab is exciting.

The tab is long.

We found a crab.

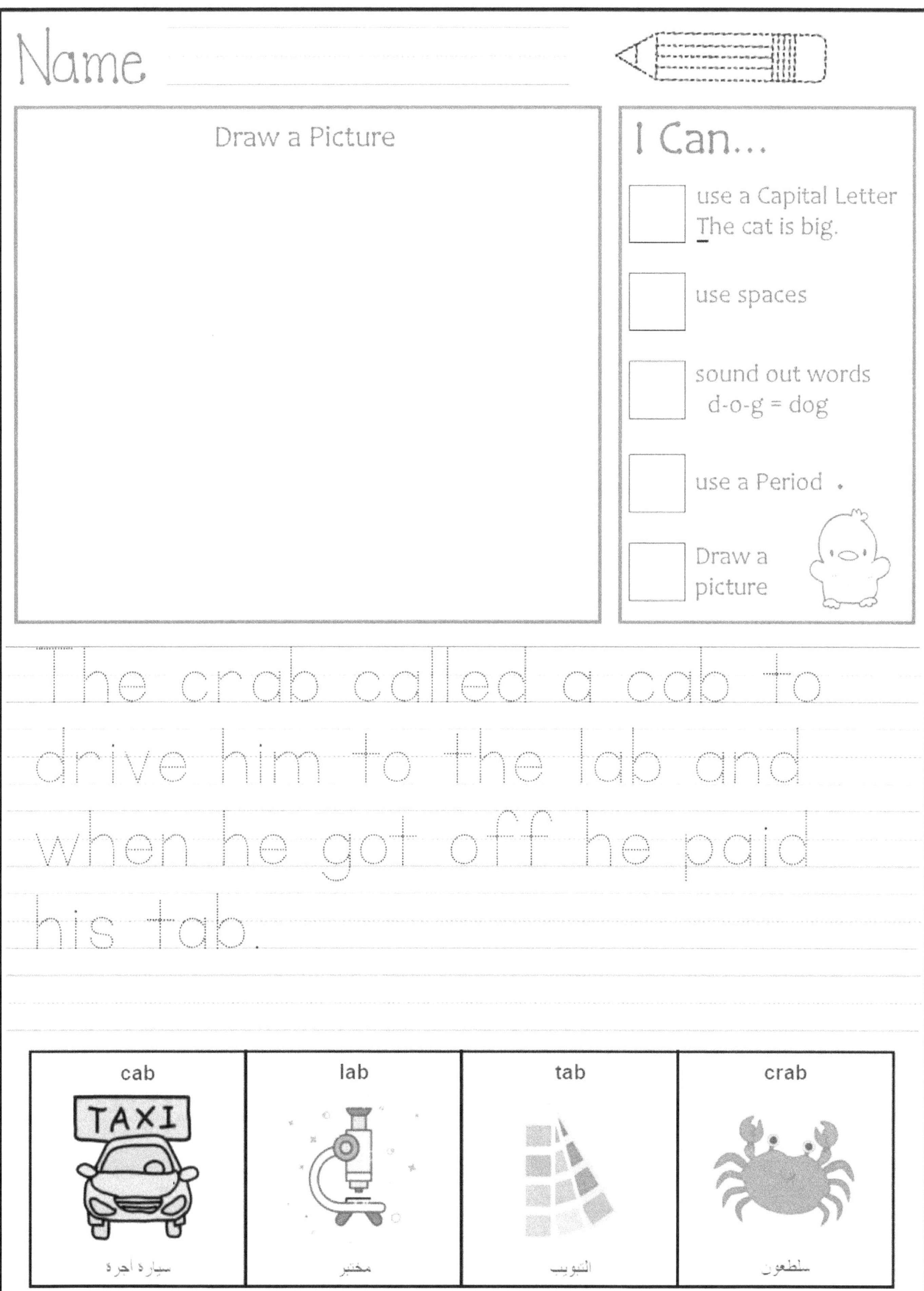

Name

Draw a Picture

I Can...

use a Capital Letter
The cat is big.

use spaces

sound out words
d-o-g = dog

use a Period .

Draw a
picture

The crab called a cab to
drive him to the lab and
when he got off he paid
his tab.

cab
TAXI

lab

tab

crab

سيارة اجرة

مختبر

التبويب

سلطعون

Name: ____________________ Date: ____________________

Today is: Monday Tuesday Wednesday Thursday Friday

Direction: Trace and read the sentences.

ham	jam	ram	clam

لحم خنزير	مربى	خروف	هادئة

I like to eat ham.

We like to eat jam.

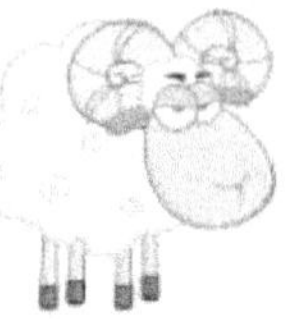

The ram is big.

The clam is pretty.

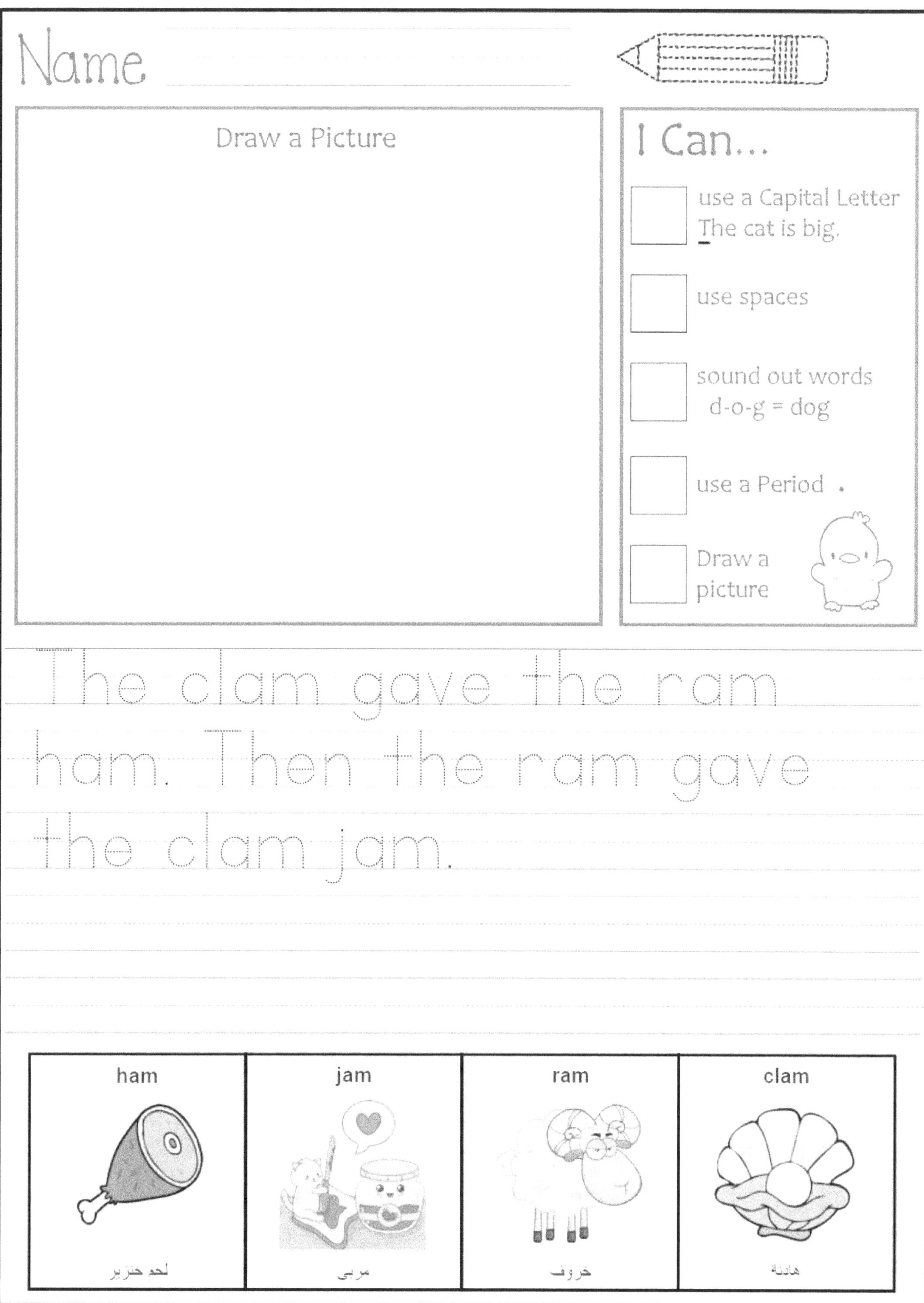

Name

Draw a Picture

I Can...
use a Capital Letter
The cat is big.

use spaces

sound out words
d-o-g = dog

use a Period .

Draw a
picture

The clam gave the ram
ham. Then the ram gave
the clam jam.

ham
لحم خنزير

jam
مربى

ram
خروف

clam
هدية

Name: ________________ Date: ____________

Today is: [Monday] [Tuesday] [Wednesday]
[Thursday] [Friday]

Direction: Trace and read the sentences.

bed	led	red	wed
السرير	قيادة	أحمر	حفل زواج

This is my little bed.

He led us to safety.

The apple is red.

He asks her to wed.

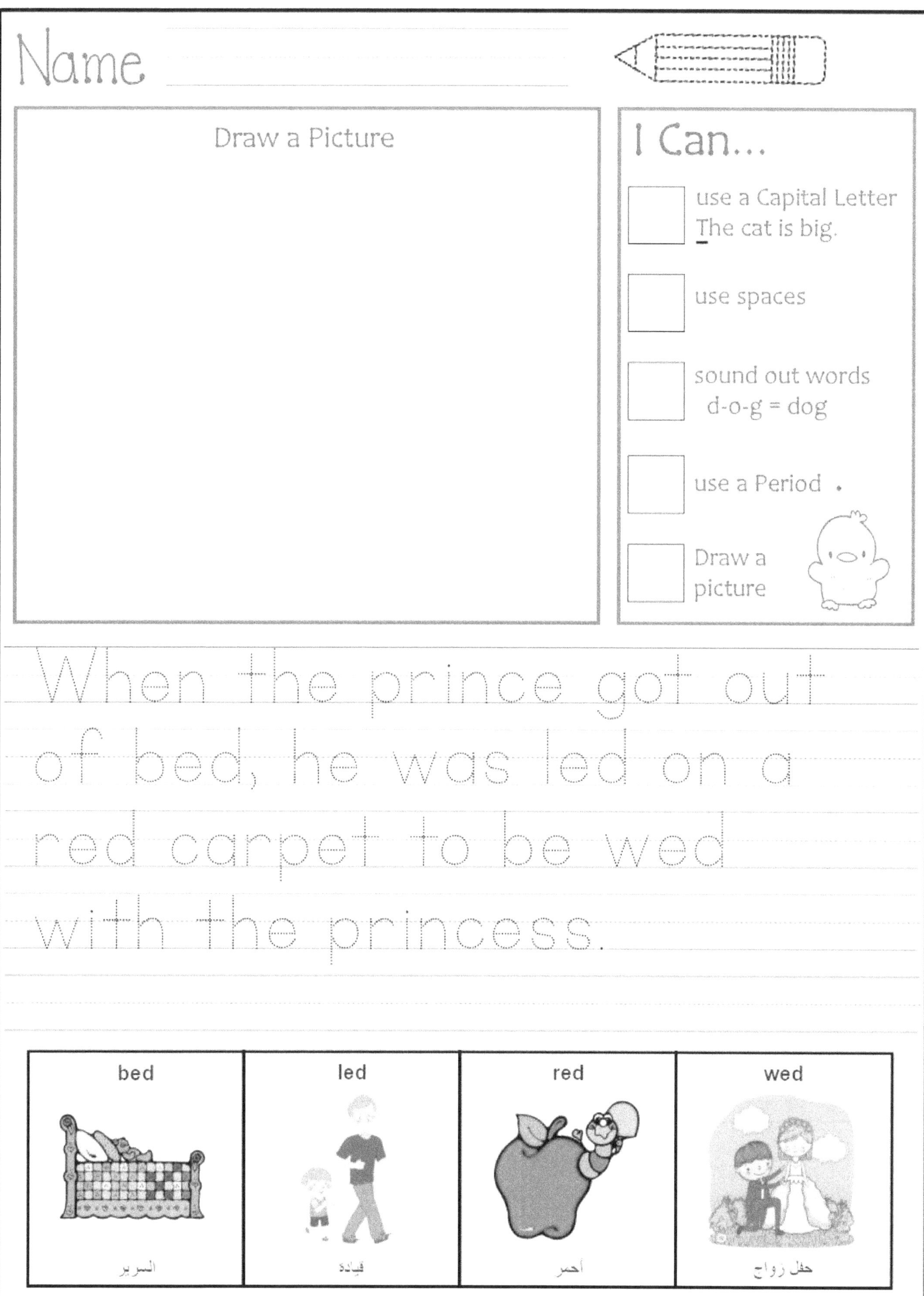

Name

Draw a Picture

I Can...

use a Capital Letter
The cat is big.

use spaces

sound out words
d-o-g = dog

use a Period .

Draw a
picture

When the prince got out
of bed, he was led on a
red carpet to be wed
with the princess.

bed
السرير

led
قيادة

red
أحمر

wed
حفل زواج

Name: ____________________ Date: ____________________

Today is: Monday Tuesday Wednesday Thursday Friday

Direction: Trace and read the sentences.

bad	dad	mad	sad

سيئة	بابا	غاضب	حزين

This apple is bad.

My dad is very kind.

The reindeer is mad.

The little cat is sad.

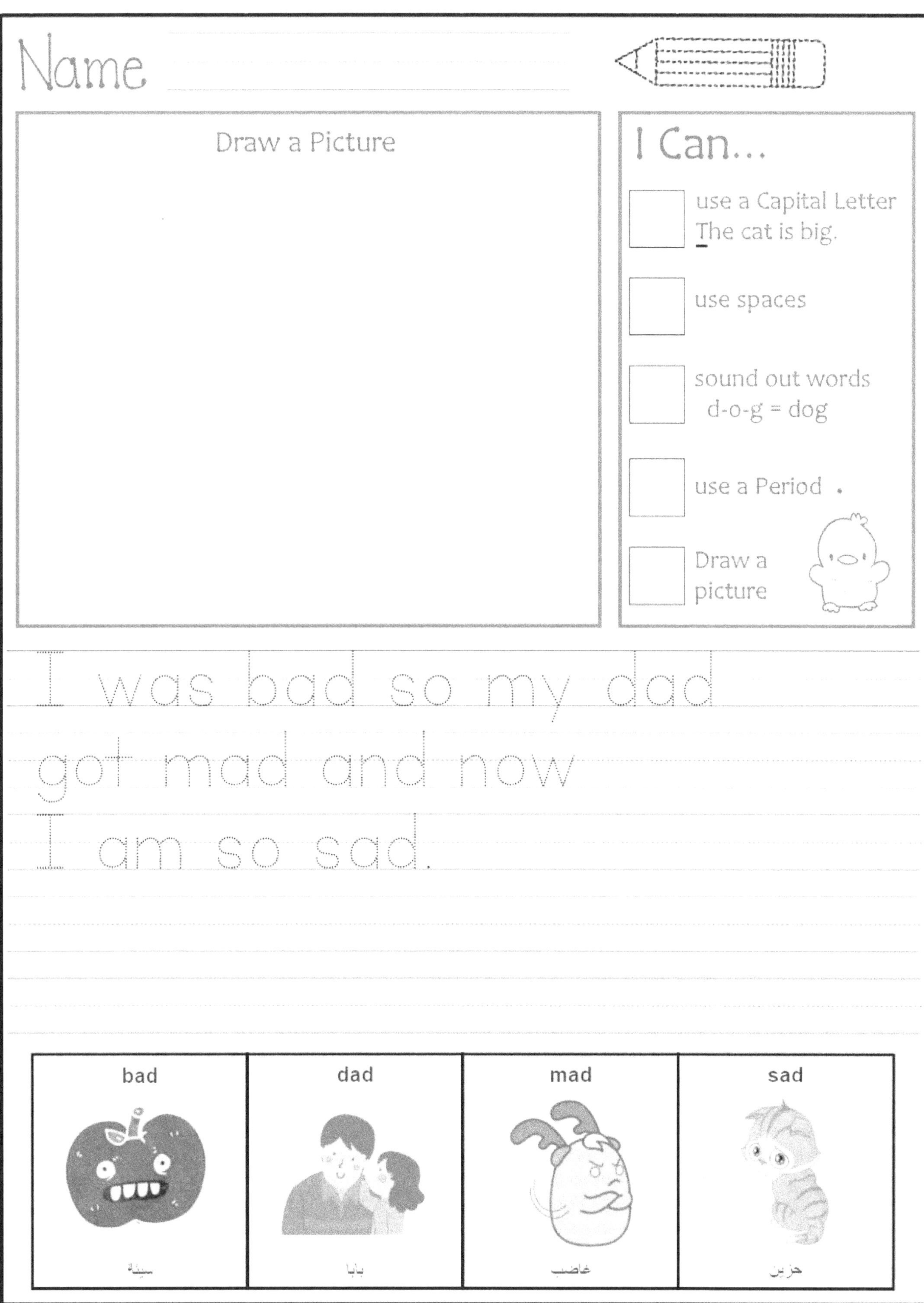

Name
Draw a Picture
I Can...
use a Capital Letter
The cat is big.
use spaces
sound out words
d-o-g = dog
use a Period .
Draw a picture
I was bad so my dad
got mad and now
I am so sad.
bad
dad
mad
sad
سيئة
بابا
غاضب
حزين

Name: _______________ Date: _______________

Today is: Monday | Tuesday | Wednesday
Thursday | Friday

Direction: Trace and read the sentences.

den	hen	pen	ten
عرين	دجاجة	اسطبلات	عشرة

It is a den.

The hens lay eggs.

She has a good pen.

The ten is smiling.

Name _______________________

Draw a Picture

- [ ] use a Capital Letter
  The cat is big.
- [ ] use spaces
- [ ] sound out words
  d-o-g = dog
- [ ] use a Period .
- [ ] Draw a picture

The hen that lived in the
pen laid ten eggs
in her den.

den	hen	pen	ten
عرين	دجاجة	اسطبلات	عشرة

Name: _________________ Date: _________

Today is: Monday Tuesday Wednesday
           Thursday Friday

Direction: Trace and read the sentences.

gum	mum	sum	drum

I like to chew gum.

My mum is kind!

I can do a sum!

The drum is big.

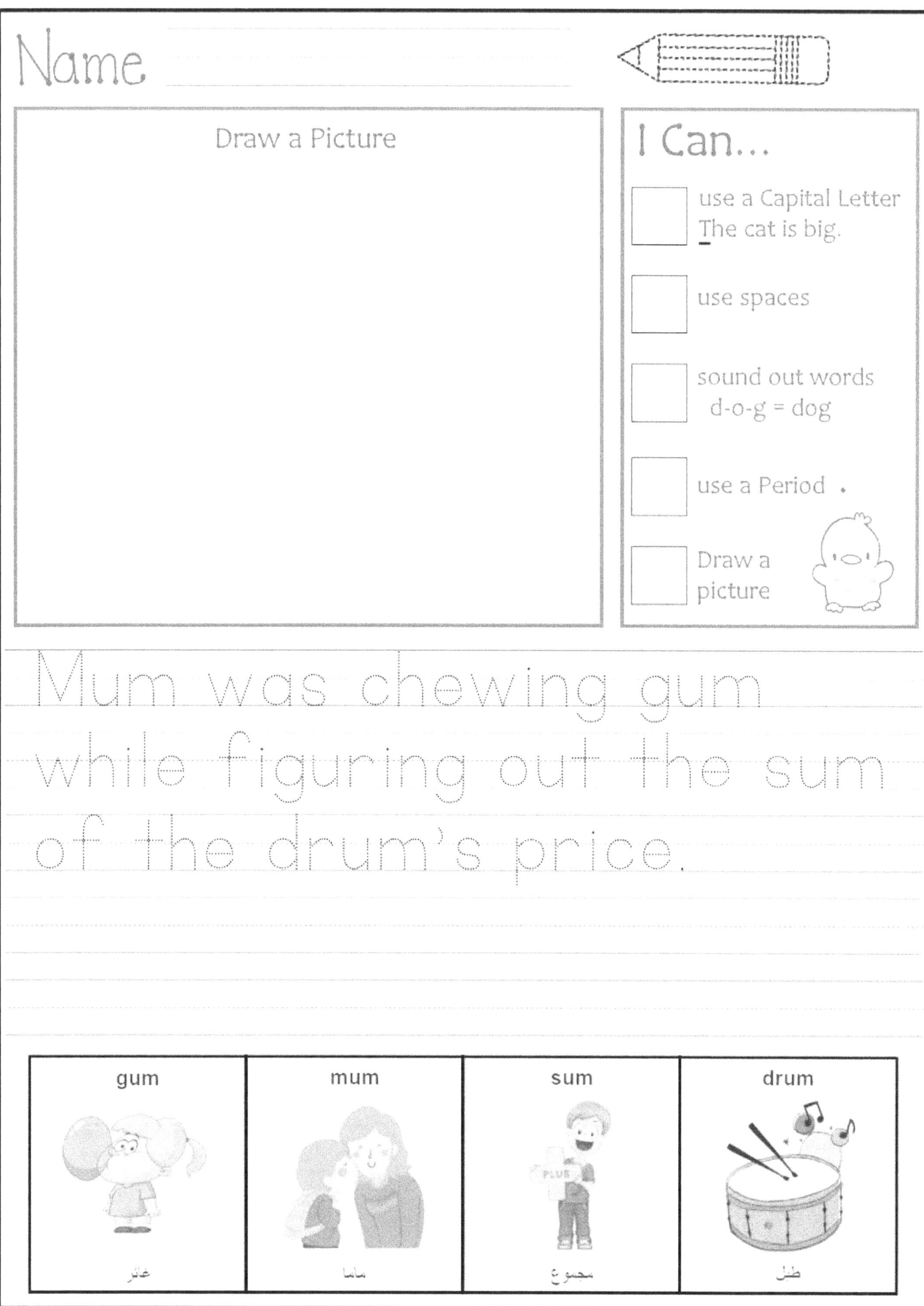

Name
Draw a Picture
I Can...
use a Capital Letter
The cat is big.
use spaces
sound out words
d-o-g = dog
use a Period .
Draw a picture
Mum was chewing gum while figuring out the sum of the drum's price.
gum
mum
sum
drum
علكة
ماما
مجموع
طبل

Name: ______________________ Date: ______________________

Today is: Monday Tuesday Wednesday Thursday Friday

Direction: Trace and read the sentences.

bid	hid	kid	lid
			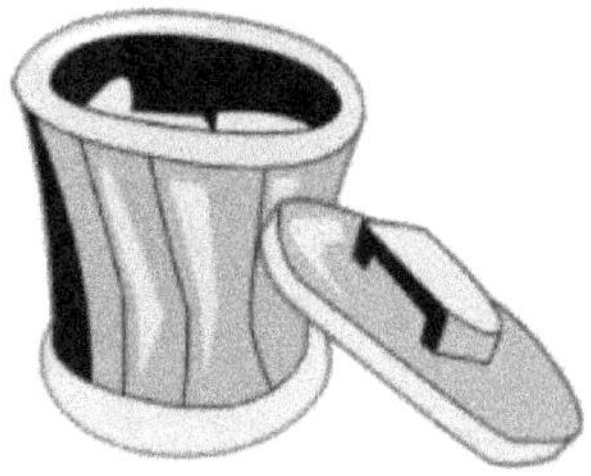
المناقصة	إخفاء	طفل	جفن العين

 He likes to bid.

 He is hiding.

 The kid like to play.

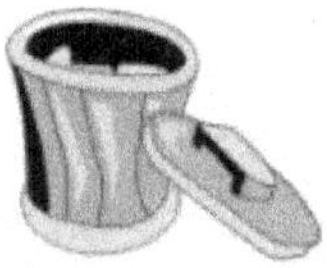 I see a lid.

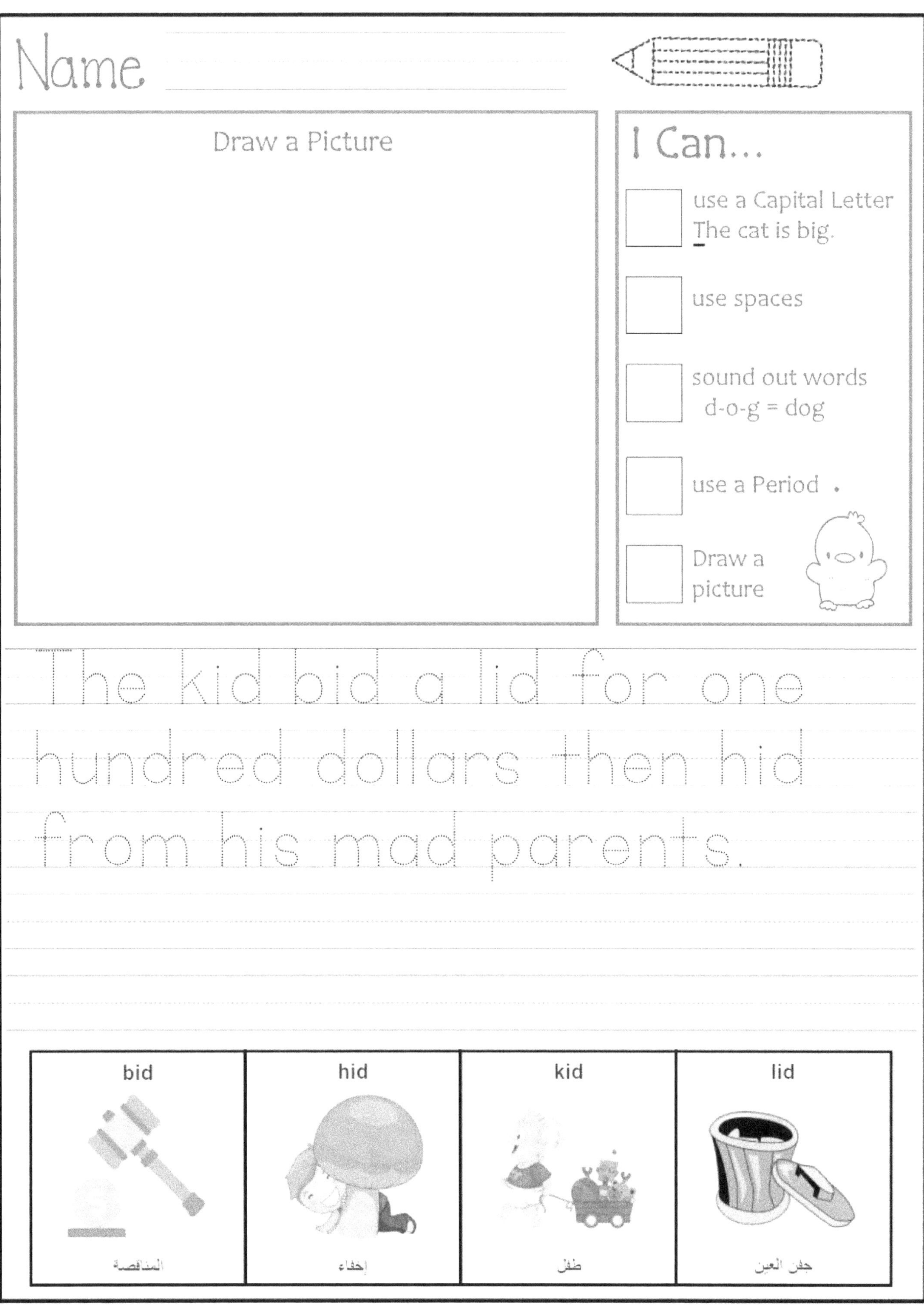

Name
Draw a Picture
I Can...
use a Capital Letter
The cat is big.
use spaces
sound out words
d-o-g = dog
use a Period .
Draw a picture
The kid bid a lid for one hundred dollars then hid from his mad parents.
bid
hid
kid
lid
المزايدة
إخفاء
طفل
جفن العين

Name: ____________________ Date: ____________________

Today is: Monday Tuesday Wednesday Thursday Friday

Direction: Trace and read the sentences.

big	dig	pig	wig

كبير	حفر	خنزير	شعر مستعار

 That is a big pencil.

 He will dig up a hole.

 The pig is fat.

 She puts on a wig.

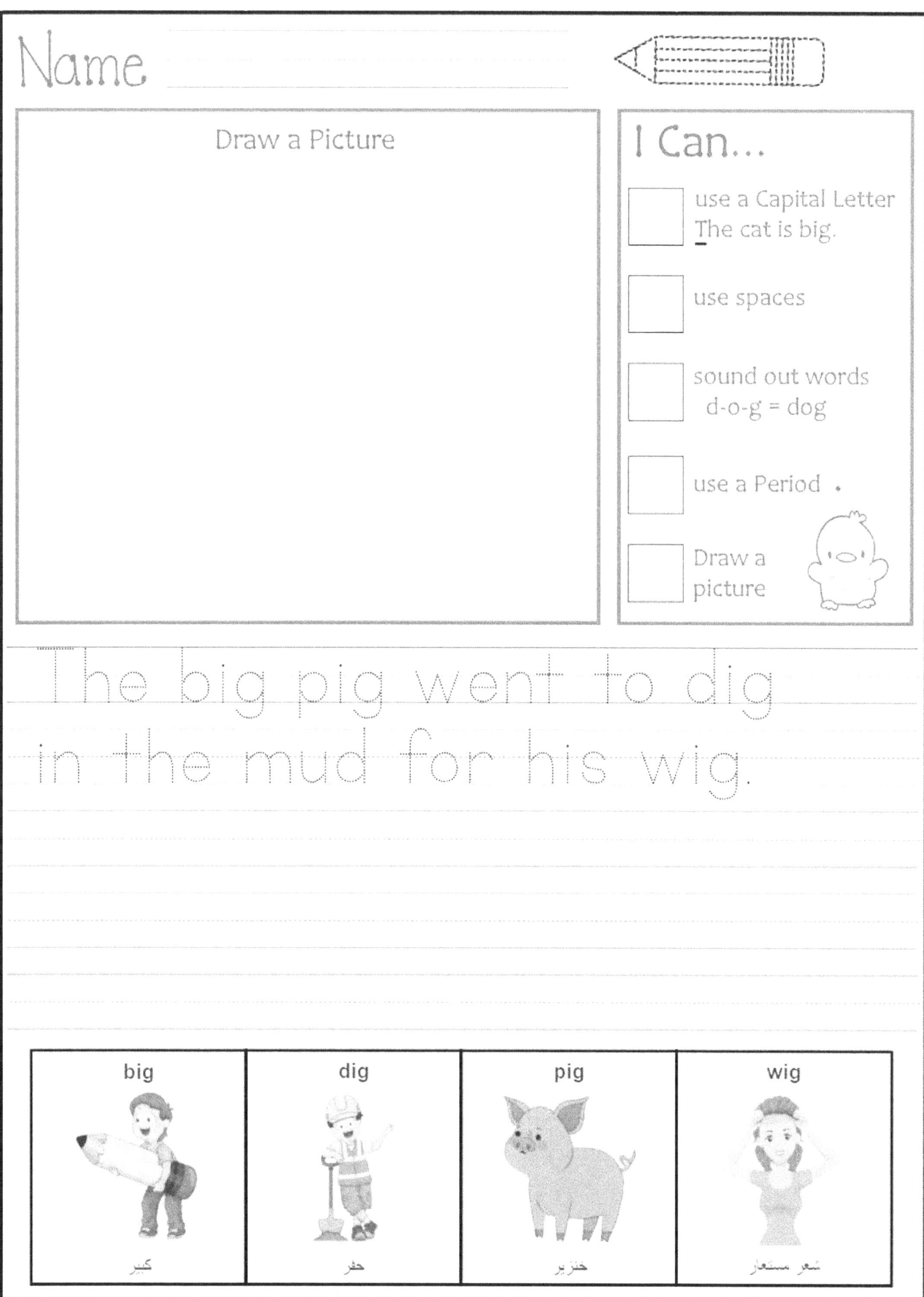

Name
Draw a Picture
I Can...
use a Capital Letter
The cat is big.
use spaces
sound out words
d-o-g = dog
use a Period .
Draw a picture
The big pig went to dig in the mud for his wig.
big
كبير
dig
حفر
pig
خنزير
wig
شعر مستعار

Name: _________________ Date: _____________

Today is: [Monday] [Tuesday] [Wednesday]
[Thursday] [Friday]

Direction: Trace and read the sentences.

bin	fin	pin	win
سلة مهملات	زعنفة	دبوس	يفوز

It is a recycle bin.

The shark has a fin.

The pin is pointy.

He won the match.

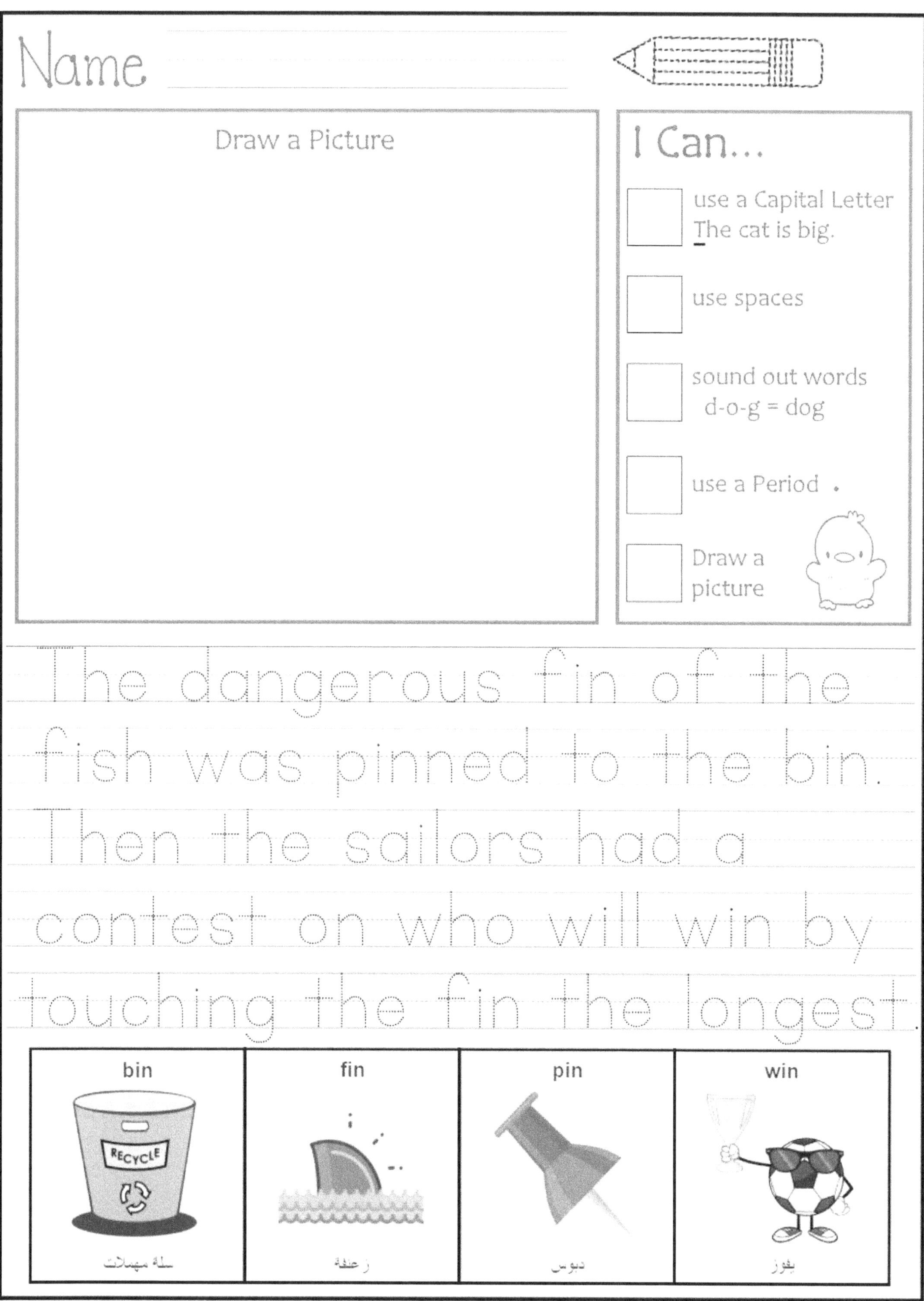

bin	fin	pin	win
سلة مهملات	زعنفة	دبوس	يفوز

Name: ____________________ Date: ____________________

Today is: Monday | Tuesday | Wednesday | Thursday | Friday

Direction: Trace and read the sentences.

hip

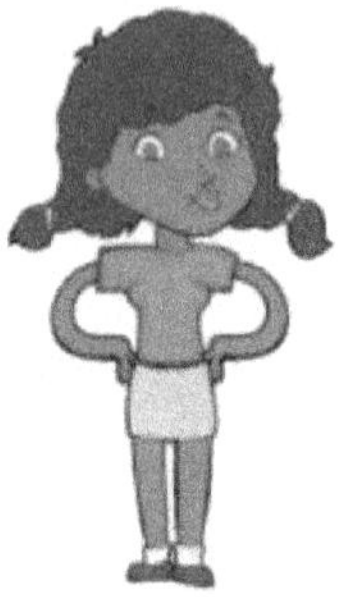

ورك او نتوء

lip

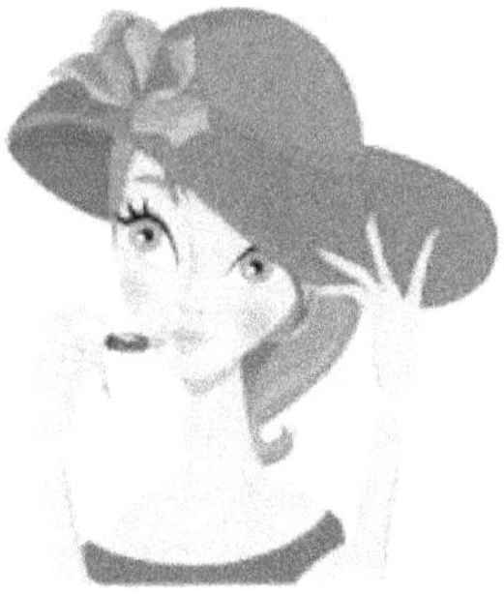

الشفاه

nip

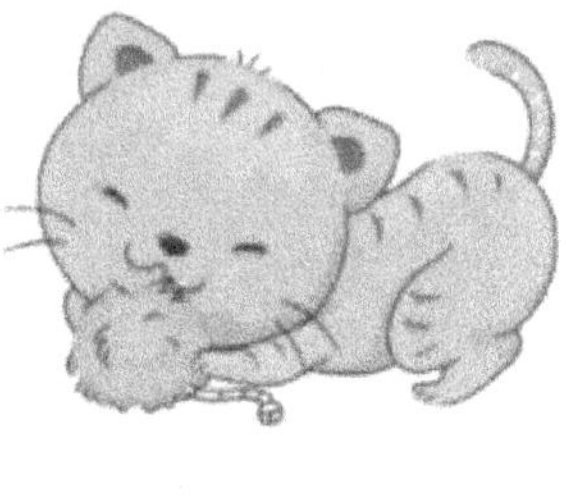

ارتشف

sip

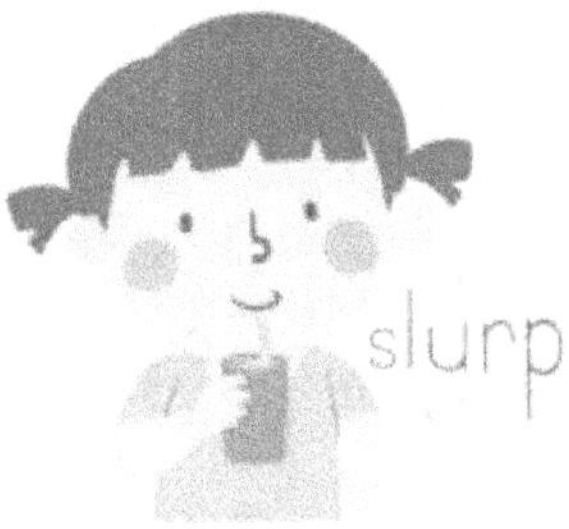

يشرب

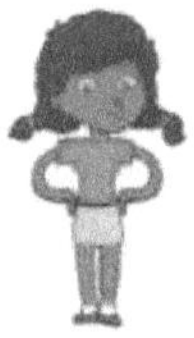

This is my hip.

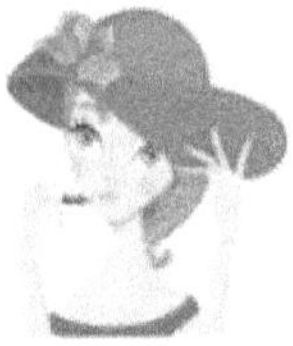

Her lips are red.

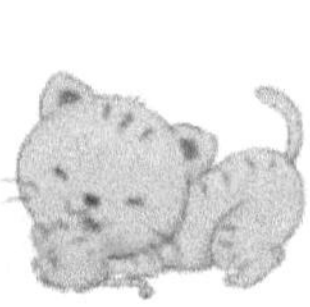

It is nipping its toy.

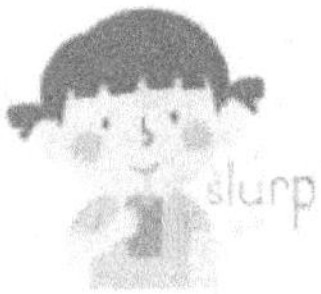

She is sipping.

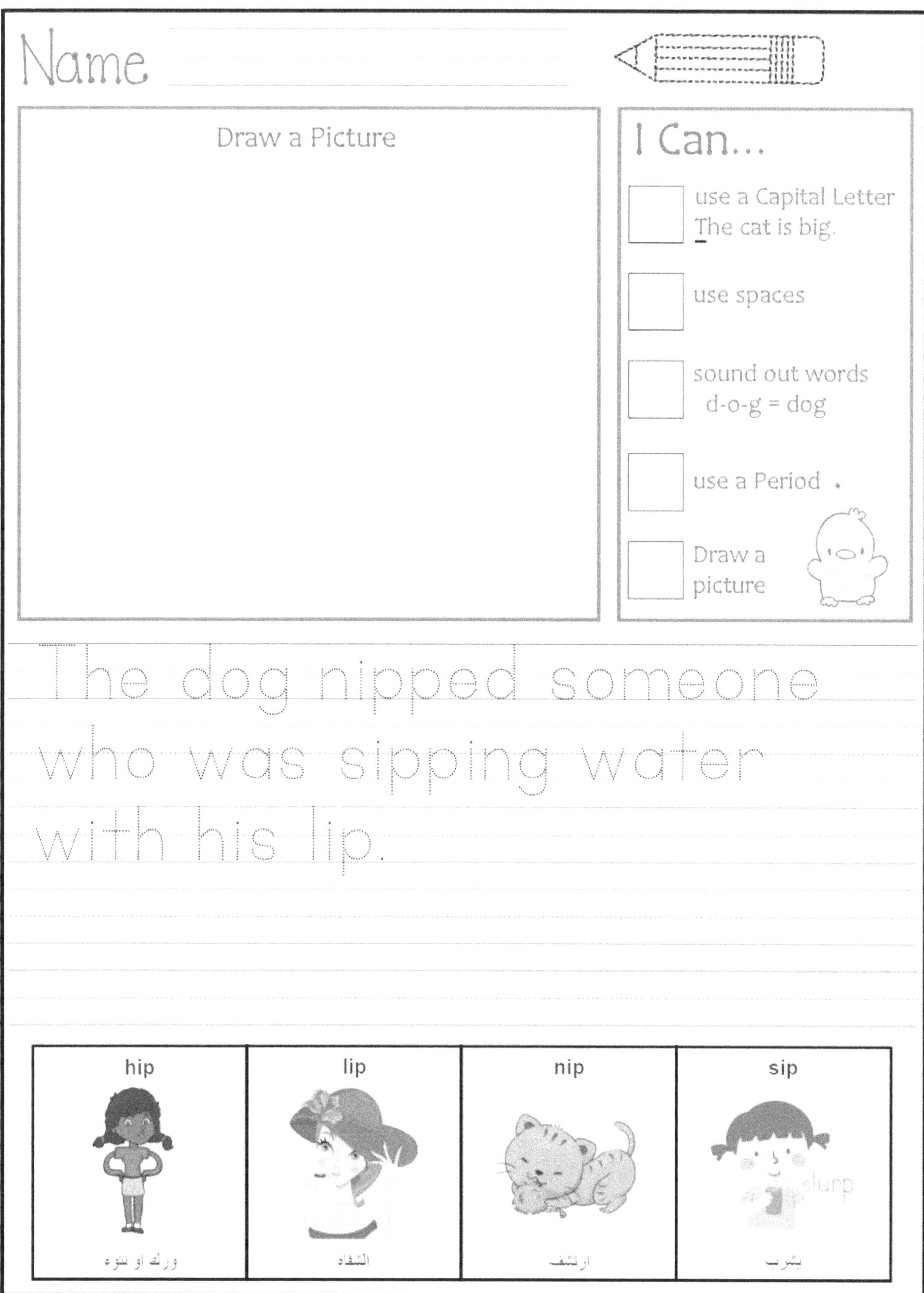

Name

Draw a Picture

I Can...

use a Capital Letter
The cat is big.

use spaces

sound out words
d-o-g = dog

use a Period .

Draw a
picture

The dog nipped someone
who was sipping water
with his lip.

hip

lip

nip

sip

slurp

ورك او نتوء

الشفاه

ارتشف

يشرب

Name: ______________________ Date: ______________________

Today is: Monday | Tuesday | Wednesday | Thursday | Friday

Direction: Trace and read the sentences.

fit	hit	kit	sit
		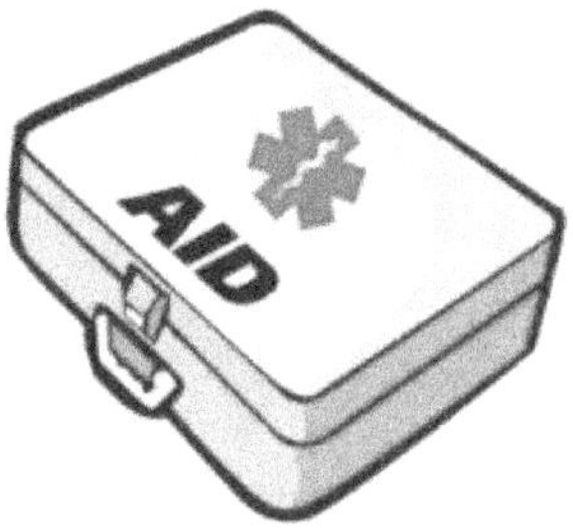	
لائق بدنيا	نجاح	عدة	تجلس

It is perfectly fit.

They hit each other.

That is a safety kit.

He is sitting.

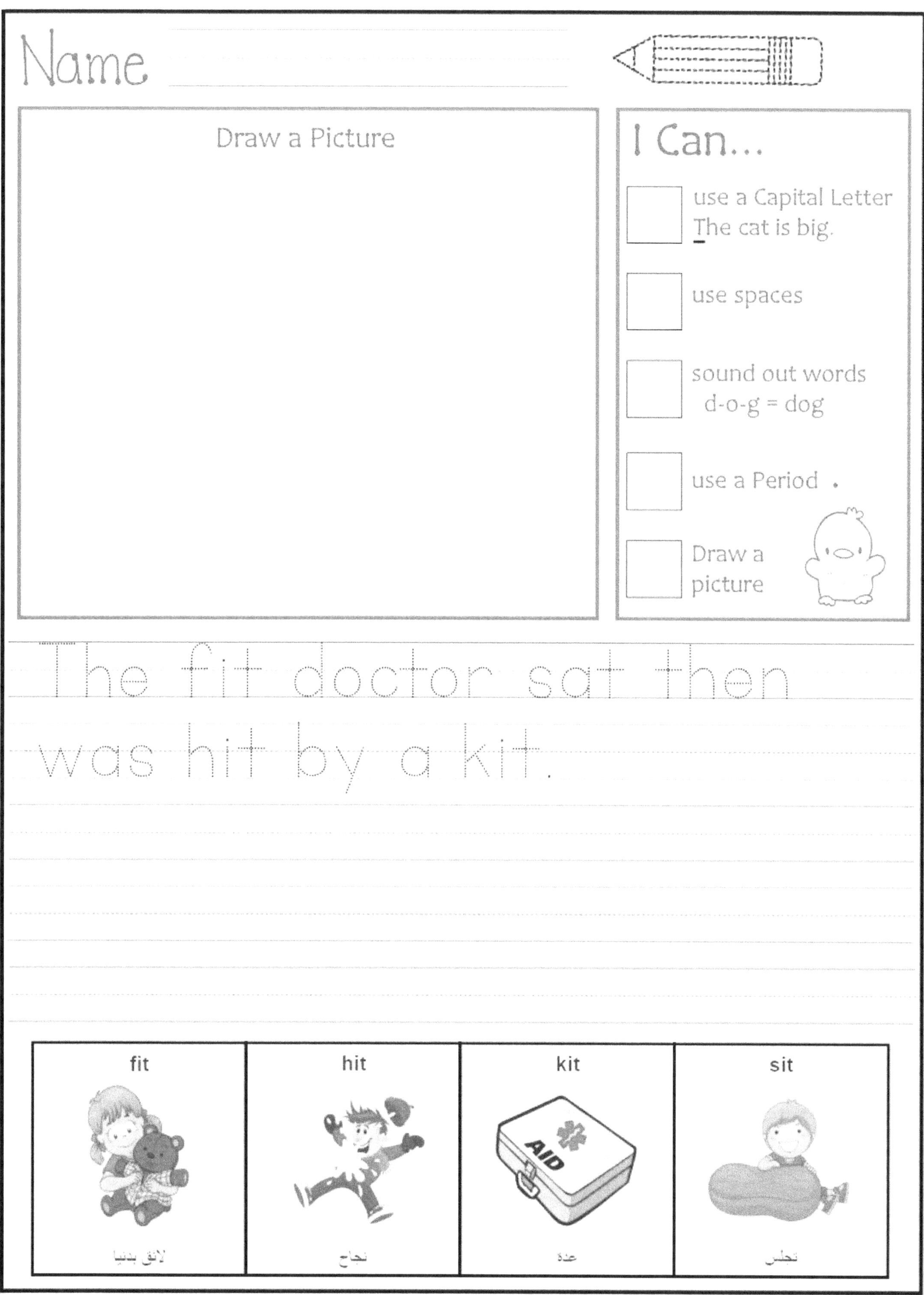

Name

Draw a Picture

I Can...

use a Capital Letter
The cat is big.

use spaces

sound out words
d-o-g = dog

use a Period .

Draw a
picture

The fit doctor sat then
was hit by a kit.

fit
لائق بدنيا

hit
نجاح

kit
عدة

sit
نجلس

cob	job	rob	sob
حبوب ذرة	مهنة	سرقة	يبكي

I ate corn on the cob.

This is my job.

He is robbing.

The girl is sobbing.

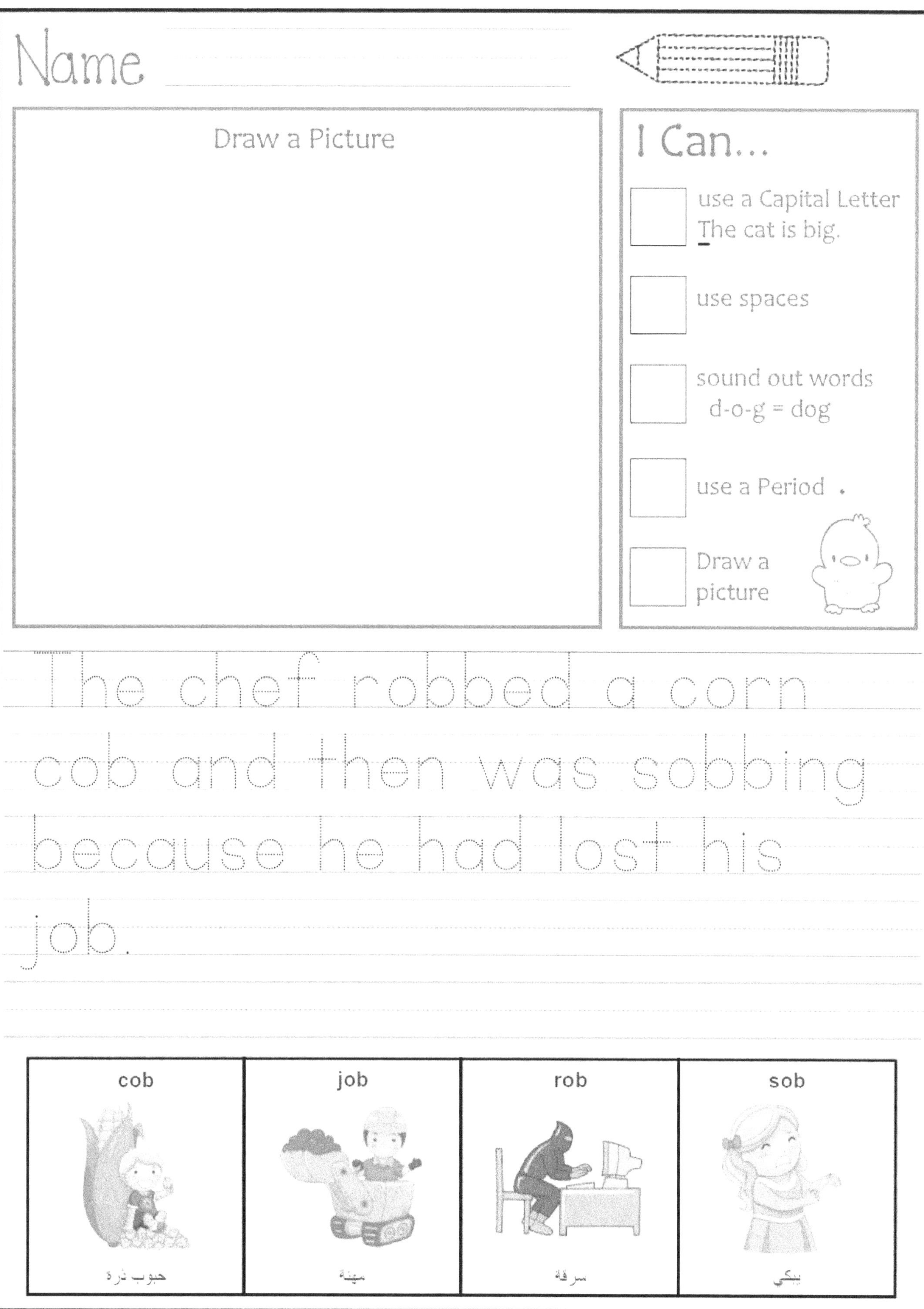

Name ______________________

Draw a Picture

I Can...

- ☐ use a Capital Letter
  <u>T</u>he cat is big.
- ☐ use spaces
- ☐ sound out words
  d-o-g = dog
- ☐ use a Period .
- ☐ Draw a picture

The chef robbed a corn cob and then was sobbing because he had lost his job.

cob	job	rob	sob
حبوب ذرة	مهنة	سرقة	يبكي

Name: ___________________ Date: _______________

Today is: Monday Tuesday Wednesday
          Thursday Friday

Direction: Trace and read the sentences.

dog	hog	jog	log
الكلب	خنزير	الركض	خشب

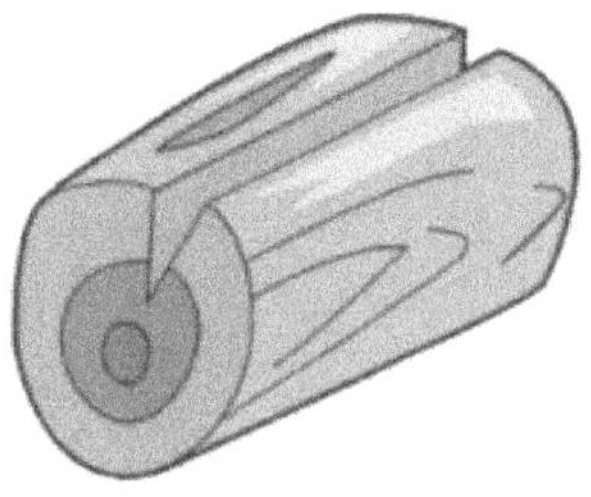

The dog is thrilled.

The hog is big.

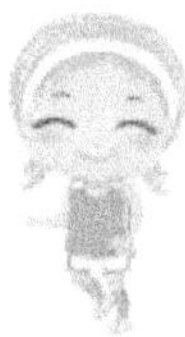

She is jogging.

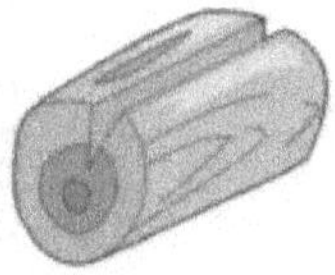

The log is small.

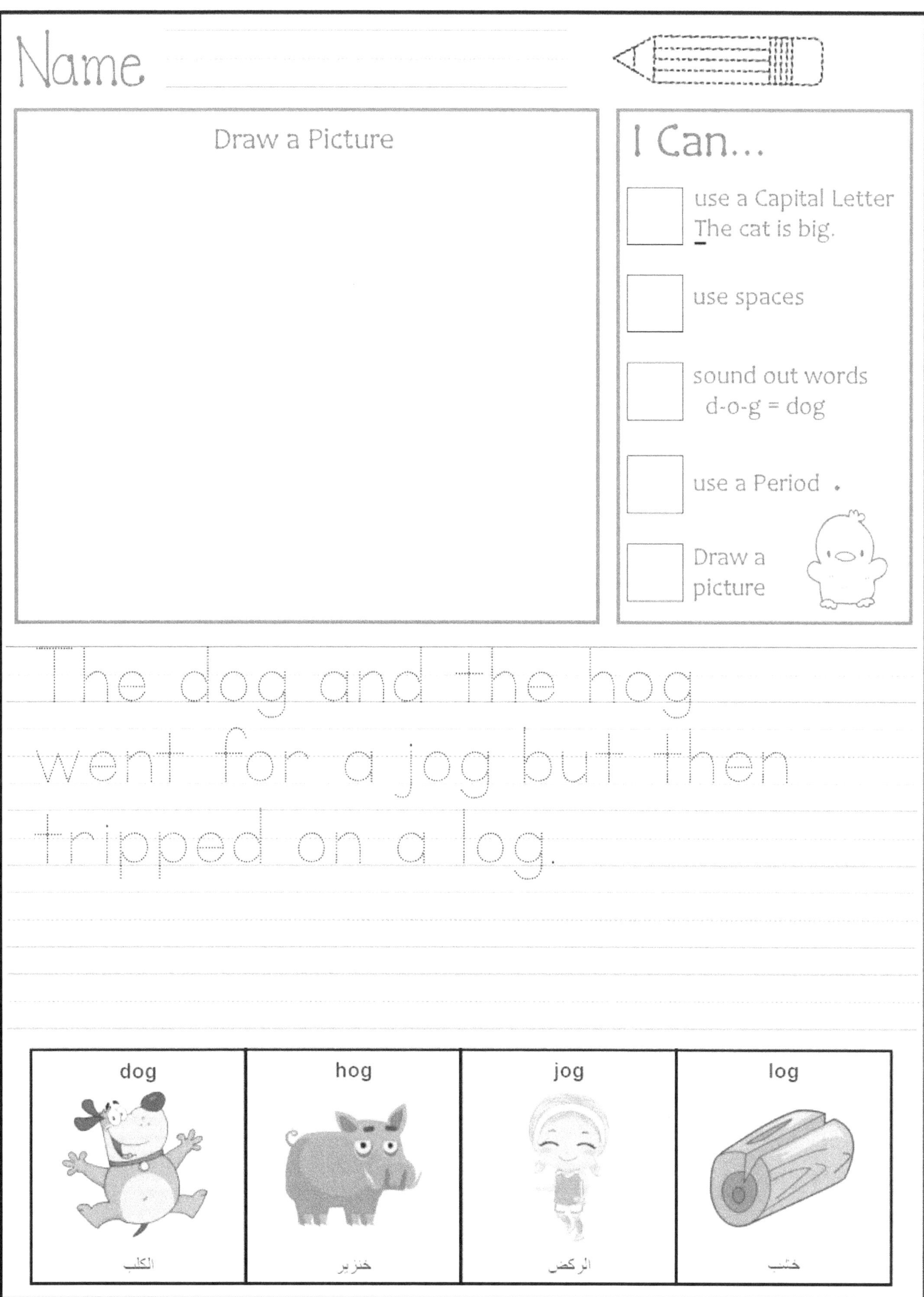

Name

Draw a Picture

I Can...

use a Capital Letter
The cat is big.

use spaces

sound out words
d-o-g = dog

use a Period .

Draw a
picture

The dog and the hog went for a jog but then tripped on a log.

dog
الكلب

hog
خنزير

jog
الركض

log
خشب

Name: ____________________ Date: ____________________

Today is: Monday Tuesday Wednesday Thursday Friday

Direction: Trace and read the sentences.

bug	hug	jug	mug
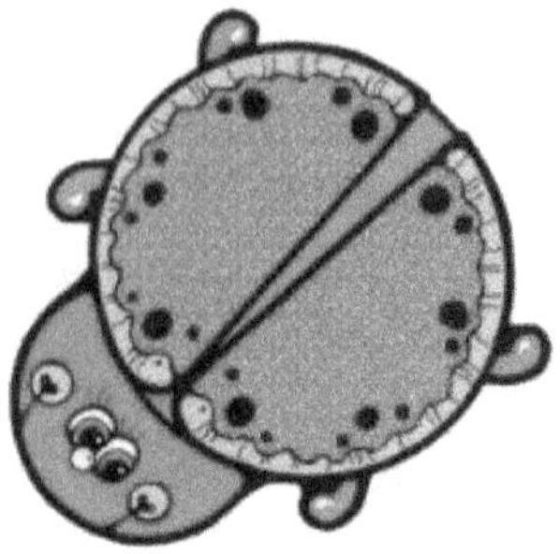			
خلل برمجي	عناق	إبريق	قدح

 The bug is colorful.

 She is hugging.

 The jug has milk in it.

 He has a mug.

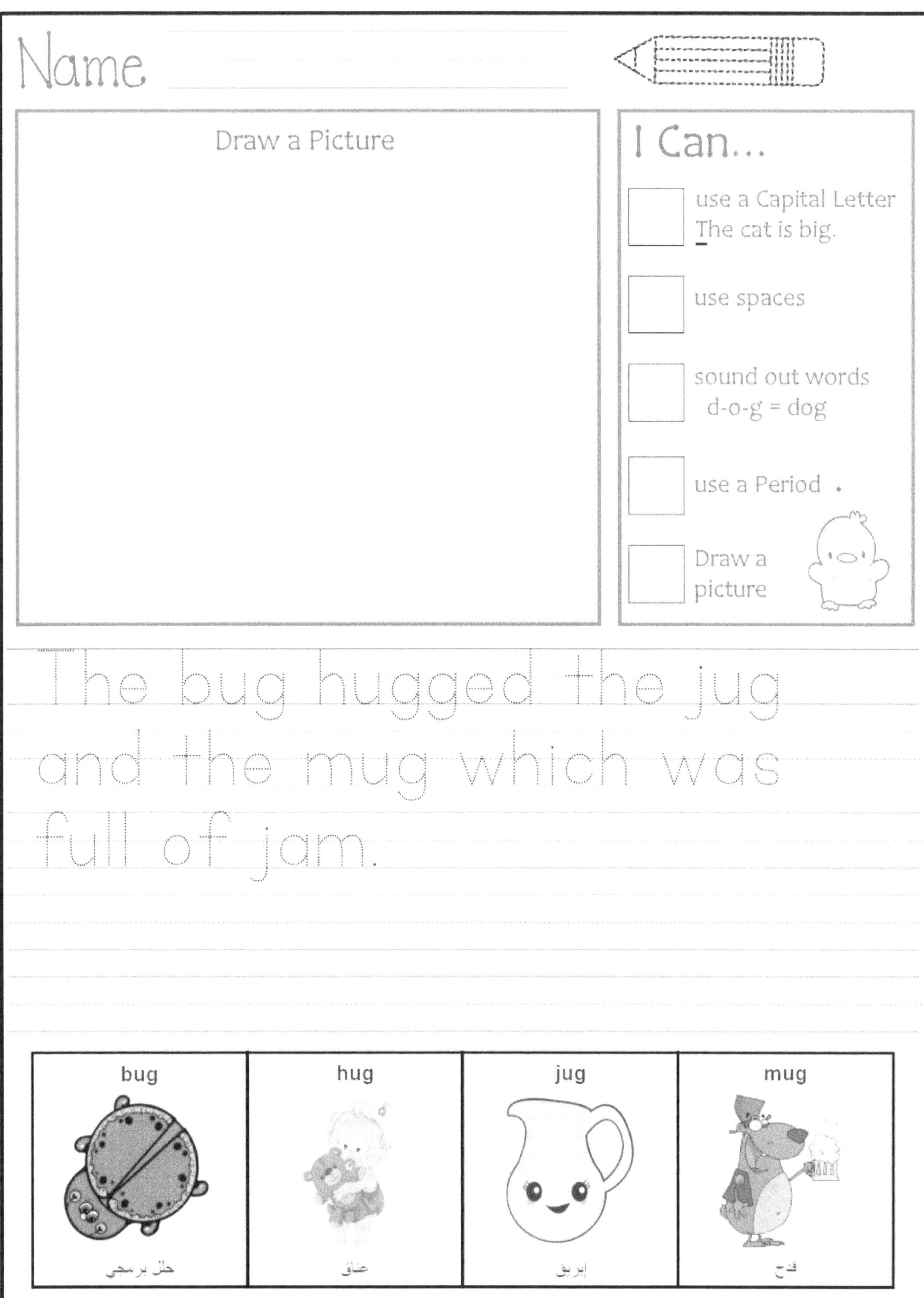

Name

Draw a Picture

I Can...

use a Capital Letter
The cat is big.

use spaces

sound out words
d-o-g = dog

use a Period .

Draw a picture

The bug hugged the jug and the mug which was full of jam.

bug
hug
jug
mug

حل برمجي
عناق
إبريق
قدح

Name: _______________ Date: _______________

Today is: Monday Tuesday Wednesday
Thursday Friday

Direction: Trace and read the sentences.

cot	dot	hot	pot
السرير	نَقطَة	الحار	وِعاء

This is my cot.

There are many dots.

It is very hot.

He has a plant pot.

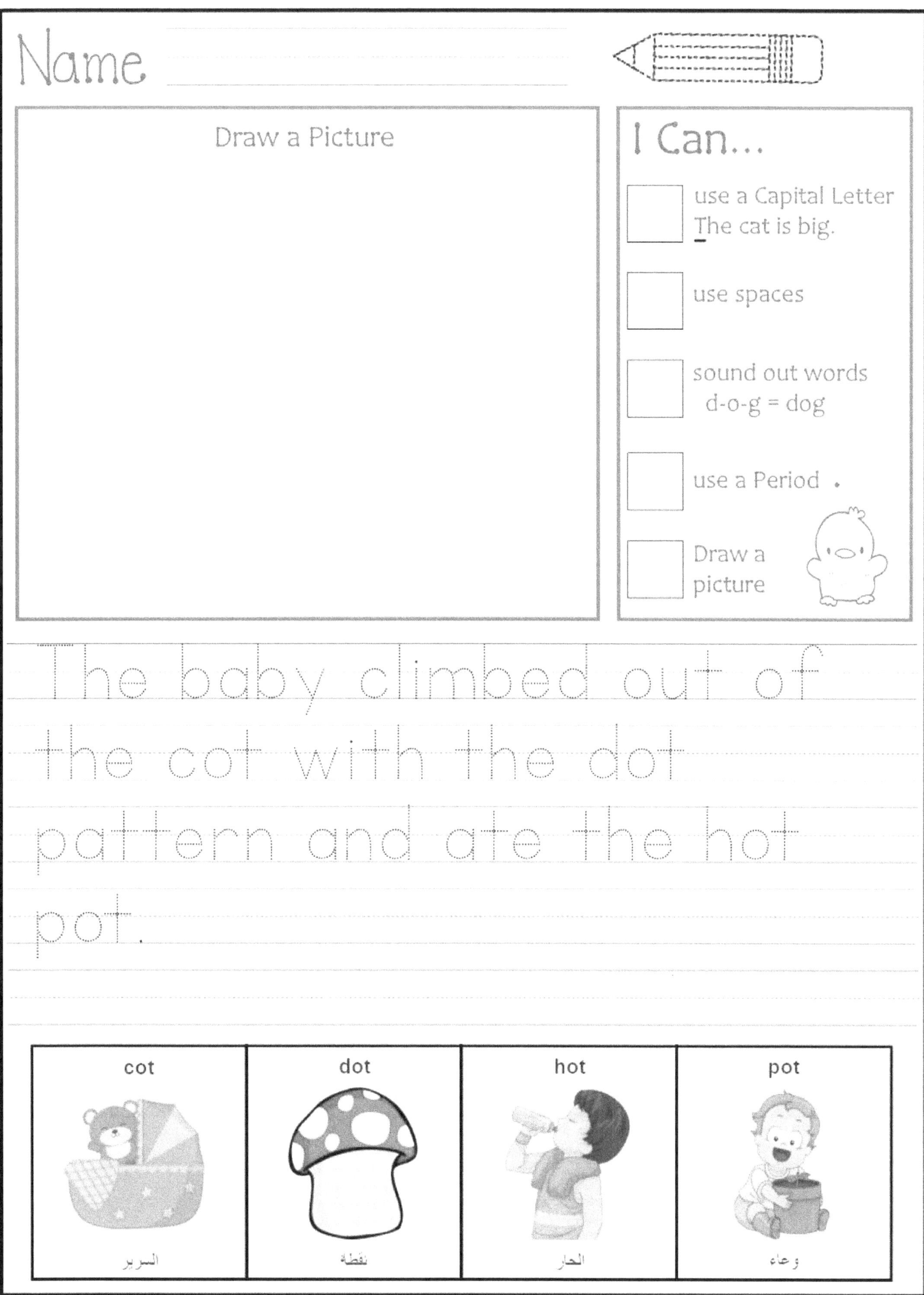

Name
Draw a Picture
I Can...
use a Capital Letter
The cat is big.
use spaces
sound out words
d-o-g = dog
use a Period .
Draw a picture
The baby climbed out of the cot with the dot pattern and ate the hot pot.
cot
dot
hot
pot
السرير
نقطة
الحار
وعاء

Name: _________________________ Date: _________________

Today is: | Monday | Tuesday | Wednesday |
| Thursday | Friday |

Direction: Read the words and make a sentence.

fun	gun	run	sun
استمع	بندقية	يركض	شمس

Name

Draw a Picture

I Can...

[ ] use a Capital Letter
<u>T</u>he cat is big.

[ ] use spaces

[ ] sound out words
d-o-g = dog

[ ] use a Period .

[ ] Draw a
picture

Name: _______________________ Date: _______________

Today is: Monday Tuesday Wednesday Thursday Friday

Name: _________________________ Date: _______________

Today is: Monday Tuesday Wednesday Thursday Friday

Direction: Read the words and make a sentence.

bag	rag	tag	wag
كيس	حرفة	بطاقة شعار	بير

Name

Draw a Picture

I Can...

- [ ] use a Capital Letter
  The cat is big.

- [ ] use spaces

- [ ] sound out words
  d-o-g = dog

- [ ] use a Period .

- [ ] Draw a picture

Name: _______________   Date: _______________

Today is: Monday Tuesday Wednesday

Thursday Friday

Name: _________________________ Date: _______________

Today is: Monday   Tuesday   Wednesday

Thursday   Friday

Direction: Read the words and make a sentence.

can	man	pan	van
علب	رجل	مقلاة	سيارة نقل

Name _______________________

Draw a Picture

I Can...

- [ ] use a Capital Letter
  The cat is big.

- [ ] use spaces

- [ ] sound out words
  d-o-g = dog

- [ ] use a Period .

- [ ] Draw a picture

Name: _______________ Date: _______________

Today is: Monday Tuesday Wednesday Thursday Friday

Name: _______________________ Date: _______________

Today is: | Monday | Tuesday | Wednesday |
| Thursday | Friday |

Direction: Read the words and make a sentence.

cut	gut	hut	nut
يقطع	أمعاء	كوخ	البندق

Name

Draw a Picture

I Can...

- [ ] use a Capital Letter
  The cat is big.

- [ ] use spaces

- [ ] sound out words
  d-o-g = dog

- [ ] use a Period .

- [ ] Draw a picture

Name: ______________________ Date: ______________________

Today is:

Monday | Tuesday | Wednesday

Thursday | Friday

Name: _________________________ Date: _________________

Today is: Monday   Tuesday   Wednesday
           Thursday   Friday

Direction: Read the words and make a sentence.

fat	cat	hat	mat
سمين	قطة	قبعة	حصيرة

Name ______________________

Draw a Picture

I Can...

☐ use a Capital Letter
The cat is big.

☐ use spaces

☐ sound out words
d-o-g = dog

☐ use a Period .

☐ Draw a picture

Name: _______________   Date: _______________

Today is: Monday   Tuesday   Wednesday
          Thursday   Friday

Name: _______________________ Date: _______________

Today is:

| Monday | Tuesday | Wednesday |

| Thursday | Friday |

Direction: Read the words and make a sentence.

cab	lab	tab	crab
سيارة أجرة	مختبر	التبويب	سلطعون

Name

Draw a Picture

I Can...

- [ ] use a Capital Letter
  The cat is big.

- [ ] use spaces

- [ ] sound out words
  d-o-g = dog

- [ ] use a Period .

- [ ] Draw a picture

Name: ___________________   Date: ___________________

Today is:

Monday   Tuesday   Wednesday

Thursday   Friday

Name: _______________________ Date: _______________________

Today is: Monday Tuesday Wednesday

Thursday Friday

Direction: Read the words and make a sentence.

ham	jam	ram	clam
لحم خنزير	مربى	خروف	هادئة

Name

Draw a Picture

I Can...

use a Capital Letter
The cat is big.

use spaces

sound out words
d-o-g = dog

use a Period .

Draw a
picture

Name: ______________________ Date: ______________________

Today is: Monday   Tuesday   Wednesday

Thursday   Friday

Name: _______________   Date: _______________

Today is: [Monday] [Tuesday] [Wednesday]
           [Thursday] [Friday]

Direction: Read the words and make a sentence.

bed	led	red	wed
السرير	قيادة	أحمر	حفل زواج

Name

Draw a Picture

I Can...

- [ ] use a Capital Letter
  The cat is big.

- [ ] use spaces

- [ ] sound out words
  d-o-g = dog

- [ ] use a Period .

- [ ] Draw a picture

Name: ___________________   Date: ___________________

Today is: Monday   Tuesday   Wednesday

Thursday   Friday

Name: _________________ Date: _________________

Today is: Monday   Tuesday   Wednesday
           Thursday   Friday

Direction: Read the words and make a sentence.

bad	dad	mad	sad
سيئة	بابا	غاضب	حزين

Name

Draw a Picture

I Can...

[ ] use a Capital Letter
The cat is big.

[ ] use spaces

[ ] sound out words
d-o-g = dog

[ ] use a Period .

[ ] Draw a picture

Name: _________________ Date: _________

Today is: Monday Tuesday Wednesday
Thursday Friday

Name: ___________________ Date: __________
Today is: Monday   Tuesday   Wednesday
           Thursday   Friday
Direction: Read the words and make a sentence.

den
عرين

hen
دجاجة

pen
اسطبلات

ten
عشرة

Draw a Picture

Name: ___________________ Date: ___________________

Today is:

Monday   Tuesday   Wednesday

Thursday   Friday

Name: _________________ Date: _________________

Today is: Monday | Tuesday | Wednesday
Thursday | Friday

Direction: Read the words and make a sentence.

gum	mum	sum	drum
غائر	ماما	مجموع	طبل

Name

Draw a Picture

I Can...

☐ use a Capital Letter
The cat is big.

☐ use spaces

☐ sound out words
d-o-g = dog

☐ use a Period .

☐ Draw a picture

Name: ___________________ Date: ___________________

Today is: Monday Tuesday Wednesday

Thursday Friday

Name: _______________ Date: _______________

Today is: Monday | Tuesday | Wednesday

Thursday | Friday

Direction: Read the words and make a sentence.

bid	hid	kid	lid

Name

Draw a Picture

I Can...

☐ use a Capital Letter
The cat is big.

☐ use spaces

☐ sound out words
d-o-g = dog

☐ use a Period .

☐ Draw a picture

Name: _______________ Date: _______________

Today is: | Monday | Tuesday | Wednesday |
Thursday | Friday |

Name: _________________________ Date: _______________

Today is: Monday | Tuesday | Wednesday | Thursday | Friday

Direction: Read the words and make a sentence.

big	dig	pig	wig
كبير	حفر	خِنْزير	شعر مستعار

Name

Draw a Picture

I Can...
use a Capital Letter
The cat is big.

use spaces

sound out words
d-o-g = dog

use a Period .

Draw a
picture

Name: _________________ Date: _________________

Today is: Monday Tuesday Wednesday
           Thursday Friday

Name: _________________________ Date: _____________

Today is: Monday Tuesday Wednesday
Thursday Friday

Direction: Read the words and make a sentence.

bin	fin	pin	win
سلة مهملات	زعنفة	دبوس	يفوز

Name

Draw a Picture

I Can...

- [ ] use a Capital Letter
  The cat is big.

- [ ] use spaces

- [ ] sound out words
  d-o-g = dog

- [ ] use a Period .

- [ ] Draw a picture

Name: _______________________ Date: _______________________

Today is: Monday   Tuesday   Wednesday   Thursday   Friday

Name: _________________________ Date: _________________________

Today is: Monday Tuesday Wednesday Thursday Friday

Direction: Read the words and make a sentence.

hip	lip	nip	sip
ورك او نتوء	الشفاه	أرتشف	يَشرب

slurp

Name

Draw a Picture

I Can...

- [ ] use a Capital Letter
  The cat is big.

- [ ] use spaces

- [ ] sound out words
  d-o-g = dog

- [ ] use a Period .

- [ ] Draw a picture

Name: _________________ Date: _________

Today is: Monday Tuesday Wednesday Thursday Friday

Name: _______________________ Date: _______________

Today is: Monday Tuesday Wednesday
Thursday Friday

Direction: Read the words and make a sentence.

fit	hit	kit	sit

Name ______________________________

Draw a Picture

I Can...

☐ use a Capital Letter
<u>T</u>he cat is big.

☐ use spaces

☐ sound out words
d-o-g = dog

☐ use a Period .

☐ Draw a picture

Name: _______________ Date: _______________

Today is: Monday Tuesday Wednesday Thursday Friday

Name: _______________ Date: _______________

Today is: Monday Tuesday Wednesday
Thursday Friday

Direction: Read the words and make a sentence.

cob	job	rob	sob
حبوب ذرة	مهنة	سرقة	يبكي

Name _______________________

Draw a Picture

I Can...

☐ use a Capital Letter
The cat is big.

☐ use spaces

☐ sound out words
d-o-g = dog

☐ use a Period .

☐ Draw a picture

Name: _______________________ Date: _______________________

Today is: Monday Tuesday Wednesday Thursday Friday

Name: _______________________ Date: _______________________

Today is: [Monday] [Tuesday] [Wednesday]
[Thursday] [Friday]

Direction: Read the words and make a sentence.

dog	hog	jog	log
الكلب	خنزير	الركض	خشب

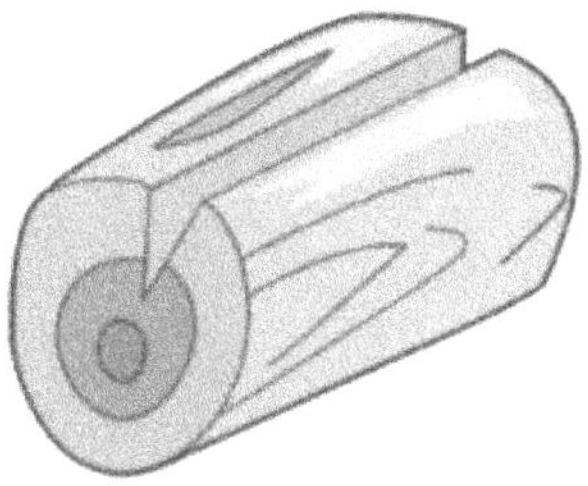

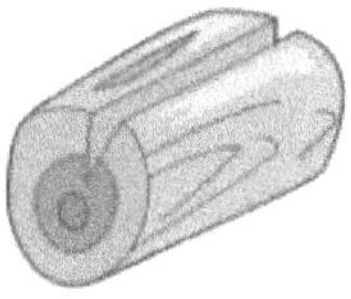

Name

Draw a Picture

I Can...

- [ ] use a Capital Letter
  The cat is big.

- [ ] use spaces

- [ ] sound out words
  d-o-g = dog

- [ ] use a Period .

- [ ] Draw a picture

Name: _______________ Date: _______________

Today is:

Monday Tuesday Wednesday

Thursday Friday

Name: _________________ Date: _______________

Today is: Monday Tuesday Wednesday Thursday Friday

Direction: Read the words and make a sentence.

bug	hug	jug	mug
خلل برمجي	عناق	إبريق	قدح

Name _______________________

Draw a Picture

I Can...

- [ ] use a Capital Letter
  The cat is big.

- [ ] use spaces

- [ ] sound out words
  d-o-g = dog

- [ ] use a Period .

- [ ] Draw a picture

Name: _______________ Date: _______________

Today is: Monday | Tuesday | Wednesday
Thursday | Friday

Name: _______________________ Date: _______________

Today is: | Monday | Tuesday | Wednesday |
| Thursday | Friday |

Direction: Read the words and make a sentence.

| cot | dot | hot | pot |
| السرير | نقطة | الحار | وعاء |

Name

Draw a Picture

I Can...

☐ use a Capital Letter
The cat is big.

☐ use spaces

☐ sound out words
d-o-g = dog

☐ use a Period .

☐ Draw a picture

Name: ______________   Date: ______________

Today is:

Monday   Tuesday   Wednesday

Thursday   Friday